CHATSWORTH REFLECTED
LEWIS NOBLE

Chatsworth Falls
2008 Watercolour on paper 20 × 20 cm

20th Anniversary

hg Hart Gallery

CHATSWORTH

Sowter Stone Pool
2008 Oil on canvas 130 × 130 cm

Introduction

I was immediately intrigued when Lewis Noble asked if he could spend a year working at Chatsworth and I have logged on to his web site frequently to see how his work is progressing. We have had two wonderful large canvasses on display throughout the autumn in the Paxton Greenhouse that runs up the hill from the Orangery shop to the stables, and I am very excited at the prospect of seeing a large number of his works exhibited together. Although the web site is first class seeing the real thing will, I know, be even more impressive.

Not surprisingly Lewis Noble has been seduced by the water at Chatsworth; not only the grand formal lakes and fountains, but also the smaller streams and the rain, of which we have had a great deal, which helps to fill them. He seems to have spent a lot of time beside the River Derwent into which all the brilliantly engineered waterworks eventually disappear.

It is not only water in all its forms that has caught Lewis Noble's imagination but, for instance, the wilder, quieter, and more private areas of the park. These are bound to have produced some fascinating work and all of this will be revealed after what I am sure for him has seemed a very short year.

Chatsworth's architecture and landscape have inevitably been painted and written about a good deal. When the first Duke rebuilt his great great grandmother's Elizabethan house between 1687 and 1707 it became a stunning statement of grandeur and sophistication in what was then a wild landscape, miles away from the centres of arts and culture. In the intervening years the world has become a much smaller place, and yet the first sight of Chatsworth, particularly from the south, is still a thrilling shock.

I am delighted that a thoughtful and contemporary artist such as Lewis Noble should have wanted to devote a whole year of his working life to painting in and around the Estate. His work will add a new layer to the impressions of Chatsworth that have built up over 400 years, and which themselves shape the way the place is imagined.

It is wonderful that the display of this corpus of work at the Hart Gallery will take Chatsworth to London, and I hope that within Lewis Noble's wide circle of admirers there may be a few people who are moved to visit the Estate. All of us at Chatsworth who have been involved with this project have been delighted with the way that it has progressed. He has reached his own conclusions and the work is there for all of us to see and to enjoy.

The Duke of Devonshire KCVO, CBE, DL
January 2009

Sowter Stone Falls
2008 Oil on canvas 130 × 130 cm

Chatsworth Reflected

Lewis Noble in conversation with John Hart

The title for your year long project "Chatsworth Reflected" seems to have several meanings. There is the ever present water around Chatsworth in which the house is indeed reflected. There are presumably your own reflections on the house and its meaning. Can you tell us a bit more about the title?

When I started the project I wanted to keep an open mind about it and let the ideas unfold through the process of painting. Chatsworth is a very diverse place in its history and landscape and I didn't want to just produce a group of 'pictures of Chatsworth' so I was very keen to develop a strong theme that could run through the year.

I had started by sketching up in Stand Wood above the house. Some of the first paintings I did were small ones of the Sowter Stone Pool and Waterfall and it occurred to me that I could follow the flow of water through the estate, from its source there, through the woods and gardens down to its entrance into the Derwent River. Water is integral to Chatsworth both functionally and decoratively and I liked the idea of the different parts of the landscape being connected by this thread. The title seemed to fit this very well, reflecting the place literally in some cases and in others more thoughtfully.

The weather this year has been remarkably wet. I remember our first meeting last winter when we could barely see the house for the drizzle, murk and mist. How has this affected your work?

In a project like this, where you are focusing on a particular place, it is easy to become involved in the very local aspects of what you are doing, so much so that you can forget to take note of the bigger picture. This is especially true at Chatsworth. It is easy to think of the manicured gardens and carefully landscaped parklands as separate from the world at large.

I was thinking about this while all the flooding was happening around the country (the village where I live suffered quite badly and some families are still recovering months later). I started to think if there was some way I could reflect this in my work. These were important events affecting the lives of people I know. I like to think that my paintings have meaning and that meaning goes beyond being just pictures of things. I didn't want to step outside of the project or to impose inappropriate meanings upon it but I must be able to comment, in however small a way, about the impact of the environment on our lives.

I was walking by the river shortly after the heavy rain. It was higher and more swollen than I had ever seen it and thundering over the weir in a deluge of noise. I stood possibly slightly too close to the edge watching the smooth, green-black river on one side of the weir become a raging torrent on the other. I thought that if I fell in there I would be swept away with no hope of swimming against it and either drown or be smashed on the river bed. Here was an embodiment of the awesome power of the natural world – beautiful and fascinating. We can tame it in many ways but in the end it will always have the upper hand and a power over life and death.

And the house, like the landscape, around it must have stood silent witness to many changes over the centuries.

Above **Waterfall Early Autumn**
2008 Watercolour on paper 20 × 20 cm

Below **Sowter Stone Falls**
2008 Watercolour and mixed media on gesso panel 35 × 35 cm

Chatsworth House itself is, of course, one of the great houses of England. It has an extraordinary presence. It is quite remarkable that such an enormous building seems to nestle in the heart of the countryside neither dominating its environment nor being overwhelmed by it. In many ways Chatsworth is its environment. Does this present a problem for you as a painter?

I am always amazed at how well the buildings seem to inhabit the landscape at Chatsworth. This is due to good design on the most part I think, but also because the landscape has grown up around the buildings. There is a sense of maturity, rather than age about the place.

In the house there is a painting of Chatsworth in the eighteenth century by Richard Wilson. On the hill behind you can see the Elizabethan Hunting Tower on an exposed moor hillside. Trees have grown up around it and it now stands in the well established mature woodland that is Stand Wood. I certainly wanted to reflect some of this sense of the house feeling like it belongs as part of the landscape and not separate from it.

As a landscape painter I am always trying to find ways to include the human element in my work. The landscape around us is all a product of human intervention. English landscape is managed by people and therefore has a human quality. I tend not to include people in my work as I like the idea of the person standing in front of the painting being the only person in the landscape. If there is someone else there they intrude on the private experience. I want the paintings to stand in for the experience of being in the actual landscape. Once there is someone there, there is a narrative whether it's intended or not. I think it's a little the same with buildings. Once you start being really specific about an object especially one as well known as Chatsworth House you start telling stories which isn't where I want to be.

I wanted to make the house part of the landscape and the way to do this came out of the project title. The series of paintings titled 'Chatsworth Reflected' is images of the house reflected from the opposite bank of the river. I like this idea as you actually have to peer *into* the landscape, *into* the water to see the house. It appeals to me as a less obvious way of showing the house and it must be an experience that thousands of people have had as they walk along that stretch of river bank. So, rather than being paintings of Chatsworth they are paintings of the experience of being at Chatsworth.

The Duke and Duchess of Devonshire have been enthusiastic for this project from the outset and we have them to thank for the help and support that they have provided. Whilst the house is in the centre of a National Park, that Park is itself surrounded by a very densely populated region of Northern Industrial towns. For many years now the Estate seems to have had a very liberal policy of access to this countryside and many visitors have a sense of shared care for this extraordinary piece of our heritage. How have the public responded to your view of their Chatsworth?

I do think that there is a feeling among the visitors to Chatsworth that it in some way belongs to them. The openness that we enjoy is certainly unique to my experience of this country's historical estates. Personally, I have been awarded very free access throughout my time here and have been assisted with enthusiasm by everyone I've encountered. I believe that this has been the case for many generations of the family and has now simply become the way it is.

I have come across many visitors in my year working here and I think I've had a pretty good response. I've enjoyed chatting to people as they pass as it makes me feel more connected. The creation and commissioning of new works of art is, after all, central to the history of Chatsworth. There is art everywhere!

Having an extended period here has given me a chance to get into the fabric of the place and beyond the appearance of certain parts of it. It's likely that what I have produced is not to everyone's taste but

Aqueduct
2008 Oil on canvas 130 × 130 cm

then nothing ever is. This is how I see it and part of the role of an artist is to show their own personal point of view and hope that it resonates with others.

Or as Paul Klee would have said "to make visible". It strikes me that this year at Chatsworth has been particularly important in your development as an artist. There is a coherence, vigour and confidence in this work. Do you feel that the project has influenced your work?

I do think that it has influenced my work and I was hoping that it would. A few years ago I spent a couple of months painting at Chatsworth as part of another project when they lent me the use of a studio. I really enjoyed that time but always felt that there was much more I could have done. I think my painting style has changed a fair bit since then and it felt like a good time to go back. When the opportunity arose I was excited to do it, partly as I always find that having a clearly defined project to work on is a big help and partly because it's such a wonderful place to go and paint.

Having the focus of creating a collection of work on one subject (albeit a large and diverse one) is very useful. There is a sense of purpose and study about each visit. My working practice for this year has been one of producing watercolour and mixed media paintings on site and then using these sketches and paintings to inform large studio work. I didn't want to have a studio there as I wanted to be working outside as much as possible. It's like having two sides to my work. I have the directly observed work, which is rapid and spontaneous reacting to what I see right in front of me. I try not to think too much and just get on with it. I never know what I've got until I get it back to the studio. In the studio it's a far slower process. I have time to develop ideas over weeks and months, make the paintings less representational and more thoughtful.

I like to think that the result is more than just a group of individual paintings but a body of work that hangs together almost to make a single artwork.

After this exhibition the work will be dispersed. How do you feel about that?

Clearly the majority of these paintings will be seen in isolation most of the time and they are individual enough to take that but I always like seeing a body of work hung together as it shows each piece in context. Having a good catalogue is a big help because it becomes a lasting record of the project as a whole. Also having the work exhibited at Chatsworth as well as in London will mean a lot of people will get to see it.

I think that there are different relationships that paintings go through. I have a very personal relationship with them while they are in the studio. This is all about change and motion. The painting is never the same to look at from one day to the next. It's like going on a journey where you know the general direction but you never know the final destination until you get there. Sometimes it can be a struggle and other times an easy path, but there's no way of knowing which it will be at the outset.

When a painting is finished it usually goes off to the gallery so I don't tend to spend a lot of time with it in a completed state. It's only when I next see it hanging in the gallery that I can be more objective about it and start to think about it as a finished painting.

I think the relationship that a painting's eventual owner has with it is very different to my own as they get to live with it for years. I like to think they have a positive effect on the lives of the people that own them.

I am sure they will have!

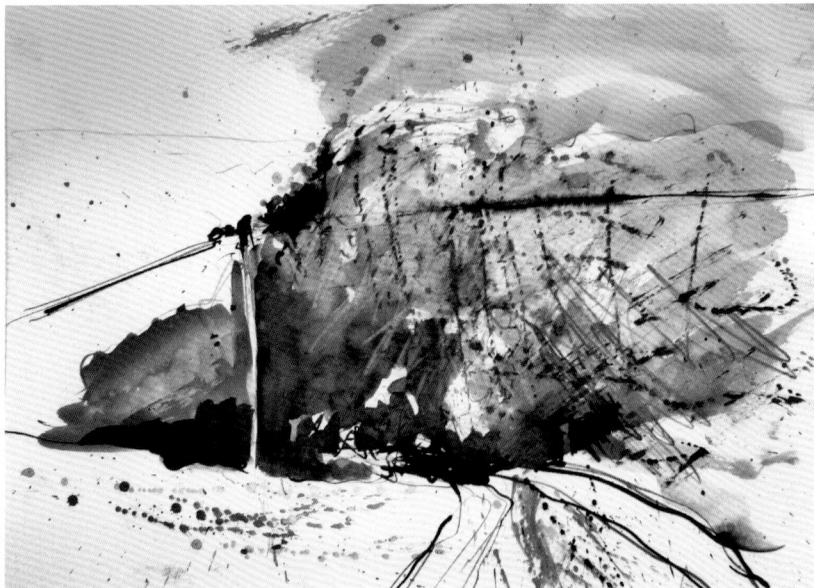

Above **From Beeley Moor 14/07/08**
2008 Ink and pencil on paper 15 × 20 cm

Below **Stand Wood 14/07/08**
2008 Ink and pencil on paper 15 × 20 cm

Above **Chatsworth, Outside Stand Wood 2**
2008 Watercolour and mixed media on gesso panel 25 × 50 cm

Below **Chatsworth, Outside Stand Wood 1**
2008 Watercolour and mixed media on gesso panel 35 × 35 cm

Above **Sowter Stone Pool**
2008 Watercolour and mixed media on gesso panel 35 × 35 cm

Below **Sowter Stone Pool (Rain)**
2008 Watercolour and mixed media 40 × 40 cm

Above **Miserable Old Day**
2008 Watercolour on paper 20 × 20 cm

Below **From Chatsworth, Due West**
2008 Watercolour on paper 25 × 25 cm

Above **Rain Coming in from Over Bakewell**
2008 Watercolour on paper 20 × 20 cm

Below **Emperor Fountain**
2008 Watercolour on paper 30 × 30 cm

Down to the River
2008 Oil on canvas 110 x 110 cm

Above **Derwent River Torrent**
2008 Oil on watercolour paper 58 × 78 cm

Below **Too Close to the Edge**
2008 Oil on watercolour paper 58 × 58 cm

Thundering Water Derwent River

2008 Watercolour and mixed media on paper 30 × 30 cm

Above **Chatsworth Reflected 2**
2008 Ink on paper 15 × 20 cm

Middle **Chatsworth Reflected 3**
2008 Ink on paper 15 × 20 cm

Below **Chatsworth Reflected 1**
2008 Ink on paper 15 × 20 cm

Above **Deluge Derwent River**
2008 Ink on paper 30 × 30 cm

Below **Weir**
2008 Watercolour on paper 30 × 30 cm

Derwent River Torrent
2008 Oil on canvas 150 × 180 cm

Above **Feel the Rain Like an English Summer**
(Chatsworth House Reflected)
2008 Watercolour and mixed media on gesso panel 30 × 30 cm

Below **Rain Spits Derwent River**
(Chatsworth House Reflected)
2008 Watercolour and mixed media on gesso panel 30 × 30 cm

Moorland Path

2008 Oil on canvas 90 × 90 cm

Lewis Noble

Curriculum Vitae

Born 1967 London

Education

1989-1992 BA Hons Fine Art, Birmingham Margaret Street. (UCE)

Selected Solo Ehibitions

2009	'Chatsworth Reflected', Chatsworth House
	'Chatsworth Reflected', Hart Gallery, London
2008	'Paintings from California', Ainscough Contemporary
	'From Where I Stand', Tregoning Gallery, Derby
2007	Hart Gallery, London
2006	'The Sun and the Rain' for Wirksworth Art Festival
2005	Hart Gallery, London
	Tregoning Gallery, Derby
	Firbob & Peacock, Cheshire
	Invited Featured Artist, Wirksworth Festival
	The Merriscourt Gallery, Oxfordshire
	St. John Street Gallery, Derbyshire
	The Ashbourne Gallery
2003	St. John Street Gallery, Derbyshire
	The Merriscourt Gallery, Oxfordshire
2002	St. John Street Gallery, Ashbourne, Derbyshire
2001	'A Sense of Place', Vickers Award exhibition,
	Derby Museum & Art Gallery
	'A Sense of Place', Vickers Award exhibition,
	Buxton Museum & Art Gallery
	Chatsworth House, Artist in Residence Open Studio exhibition
	St. John Street Gallery, Ashbourne, Derbyshire
2000	Northcote Gallery, London
	The Ashbourne Gallery, Derbyshire
1999	Ainscough Contemporary Art, London
1998	Dukes Oak Gallery, Cheshire
	Ainscough Contemporary Art, London
1997	The Ashbourne Gallery, Derbyshire
1996	Byard Art, Nottingham
	The Ashbourne Gallery, Derbyshire
	Derby Playhouse

Selected Group Ehibitions

2008	London Art Fair with Hart Gallery
	Art London with Hart Gallery
2007	London Art Fair with Hart Gallery
	Art London with Hart Gallery
	'In Situ', Tregoning Gallery, Derby
2006	Tregoning Gallery, Derby,
	Ainscough Contemporary Art
	St. John Street Gallery, Derbsyhire
	Firbob & Peacock, Cheshire
2004	The Merriscourt Gallery, Oxfordshire
	Glasgow Art Fair
	Ainscough Contemporary Art
	Firbob & Peacock, Cheshire
2003	Ainscough Contemporary Art, London
	Walker Galleries, Harrogate
	The Ashbourne Gallery, Derbyshire
	John Martin of London
	Affordable Art Fair, London
	Byard Court, Cambridge
2002	Ainscough Contemporary Art, London
	John Martin of London, London
	The Merriscourt Gallery, Oxfordshire
	Walker Galleries, Harrogate
	Battersea Art Fair, London
	Byard Art, Cambridge
2001	Affordable Art Fair West, Bath
	Affordable Art Fair, London

	Derby Museums & Art Gallery
	Ainscough Contemporary Art
2000	Affordable Art Fair, London
	Chelsea Art Fair
	Dublin Art Fair
	Tregoning Fine Art
	Art London
1999	The Merriscourt Gallery, Oxfordshire
	Gallery 108, London
	The Courtyard Gallery, Hampshire
	Affordable Art Fair, London
	Chelsea Art Fair
	West of England Art Fair
	Ashbourne Art Gallery, Derbyshire
	Art London
1998	Gagliardi Gallery, London
	Derby Museum and Art Gallery
	The Ashbourne Gallery, Derbyshire
1997	Ainscough Contemporary Art, London
	Derby Museum and Art Gallery
	Dukes Oak Gallery, Cheshire
1996	Derby Museum and Art Gallery
	The Assembly Rooms, Derby

Awards

2001	Winner, Vickers Art Award
1996	Prize-winner, Derby City Open
1995	Prize-winner, Derby City Open

Publications

2007	Hart Gallery, Catalogue essay by John Casken
2009	Hart Gallery, Catalogue 'Chatsworth Reflected',
	Introduction by The Duke of Devonshire,
	Interview with John Hart

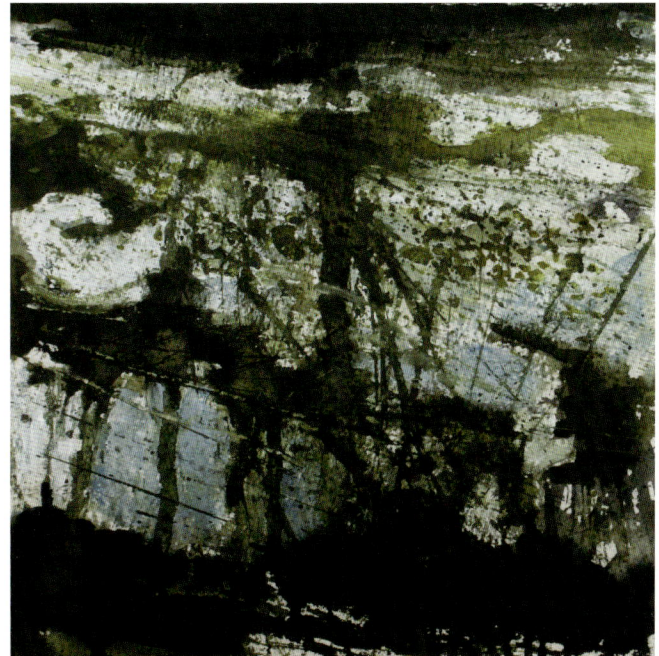

Morton Pond
2008 Watercolour on paper 25 x 25 cm

Chatsworth Reflected

Lewis Noble

Special thanks to: The Duke and Duchess of Devonshire,
Simon Seligman, Claire Fowler, David Spencer, Steve Porter.

Catalogue co-ordination: Laura Saile and Rachel Ball

Photography: Lewis and Mandy Noble

Printed: Healeys Print Group

ISBN No. 978-1-902721-29-3

Front cover:

Autumn (Chatsworth House Reflected on Derwent River)
2008 Oil on canvas 130 × 130 cm

Back cover:

Chatsworth Reflected
2008 Watercolour and mixed media on gesso panel 40 × 40 cm

Lewis Noble's work on display in
Paxton's Conservative Wall greenhouse, Chatsworth.

20th Anniversary

hg Hart Gallery

THE SOCIETY OF LONDON ART DEALERS
MEMBER

Hart Gallery 113 Upper Street, Islington, London N1 1QN Telephone: 020 7704 1131 Facsimile: 020 7288 2922
Hart Gallery Nottingham 23 Main Street, Linby, Nottingham Telephone: 0115 963 8707 Facsimile: 0115 964 0743

www. hartgallery.co.uk